Come Let Us Adore Him

Selected Scriptures with Christmas Reflections by
THOMAS KINKADE
Painter of Light™

✶ Celebrating the Glory of Christmas ✶

THOMAS NELSON PUBLISHERS
Nashville

Presented to:

Dad

From:

Karen

Date:

12/25/99

Contents

Gallery of Paintings

A Birth Foretold
THE COMING MESSIAH

Born Is the King
THE PROPHECY FULFILLED

Joy to the World
LET HEAVEN AND NATURE SING!

Worship and Praise
GLORY TO THE NEWBORN KING!

Come Let Us Adore Him
GLORY TO GOD IN THE HIGHEST!

Painting Grace

On the canvas of my mind, I see the picture clearly. A little child, clothes torn and tattered, stands lost in the heart of a deep, dark forest. As night descends, his fears arise, heart pounding as he turns to the right . . . to the left . . . and recognizes nothing. Can see nothing. He knows he is as good as dead, for it is only a matter of moments before the night creatures overtake his fragile form.

But look! There is a light in the distance, and steadily it comes closer. Suddenly the boy can see the enormous shape of a man, holding the lantern above his head. "It is the King," the boy says to himself. "And He has come just for me."

And with that, the giant but gentle King bends down and scoops up the boy in His big, burly arms. "Come with Me, My child," the King says to the boy. "I have prepared a wonderful place for you. It is a world full of light and beautiful things—a world that grows in the grace of My love. It is reserved just for you. Come, let Me show you the light."

Imagine if you were that child—the joy of feeling His arms surround you with a safety and love like you've never known. Buried in His chest there is warmth, peace, and hope. It is the message of true love, and it is the portrait of Christmas.

It astounds me that God sees me as that little boy, lost without hope in a dark and dying world. Then out of the dismal night comes His light of hope—His own Son—who saves me from certain death, and places me in the kingdom of His love.

I believe that is why so much of Christmas is defined by light. Light in the trees, on the houses, from the candles and the fireplace. The darker the night, the brighter they shine—like Christ's love on that blessed birthday. In humility He came, exchanging royal robes for swaddling cloths, and a throne for a meager manger. But all of the light of heaven filled His soul, and lit the dark world with an eternal flame of hope.

If I had been given the opportunity to be a part of that first Christmas, I believe I'd have asked the child how I could be a part of His light—how I could capture His heart in myself, and be a beacon of that

hope for others. And as if He had known just what I'd ask, He would have handed me the key to my dream through His Word.

"Receive me." To celebrate Christmas with Jesus means simply to receive the ultimate gift, the gift of life. And as I open this precious gift, His light chases away the shadows of my soul.

No wonder Christmas is such a joyous time. Yes, the ceremony and circumstance are sweet. Some of the fondest memories of my life revolve around the Christmas season, with my brother and sister and mother, playing amid the poverty and making Christmas merry. In the following pages, you'll see snapshot portraits of those times and how God used them to draw me even closer to Him. Christmas now holds special fun as I see the excitement in my four little girls. The anticipation seems the same for them as it did for me when I was growing up, even though the financial conditions are worlds apart. But each of the Christmas events we may be tempted to think of as worldly and wrong, in the light of Christ, point to a purpose much greater. They are the physical, tangible realities we celebrate each year that help our hearts understand the deeper, spiritual truths those traditions represent.

When I was a child, I saw Christmas only through the eyes of a child. It was my joy to play with my toys and with my friends on the day when all the world seemed right. As a parent, now, I get a glimpse of the joy our heavenly Father feels when He gives good gifts to His children. Though sometimes children respond wrongly—like I always did when I got clothes instead of toys—the gifts from our Father are always for our good. And His love is the reason I rejoice.

This Christmas season I hope you find the chance, amid the chaos and crazy schedules, to settle in for the night and shine the Savior's message of light on your loved ones. And in your home, and mine, God's children will discover again the joy of Christmas, for the Light of the World has come. And He shines in you and me.

A Birth Foretold

THE COMING MESSIAH

Mary and Joseph approached that incredible birth with the knowledge that something extraordinary was about to happen. The God of all creation was coming to earth—through their child—to restore the relationship between God and His people.

The Wait

*I*t was almost more than I could stand. Gifts, neatly wrapped in gaudy green and red, trimmed the bottom of the tree my brother and I had chopped down weeks earlier in preparation for the great event. We did not have a lot of money growing up in our home. Dad was gone, and mom alone worked to make ends meet. But somehow, magically, we'd find what we wanted under that special tree when the time was right.

For us, Christmas was a big deal. And in a small town like Placerville, California, this deal was bigger than any other. As a community we commemorated the season with lights, an inexpensive but essential element to creating the mood we anticipated so greatly. Some weeks before the day ever arrived, the whole town would turn out to see the giant redwood tree in the town square lit up with myriad colors. At home we'd replicate the event with our own jewel-tones, lining the trim of our home and the tree with lights. The rest of our decorations were mostly home-made, due to our limited funds, but in good taste—except the one year my mom left a can of flocking behind on her way to work. When she returned home that evening, she found every window of the house frosted with white, snowy Christmas slogans saluting the season—and every passerby. She was a good

sport, though, and left them up, thinking it might just be the

whitest Christmas our little home in the arid California climate

would ever get to see.

But as Christmas day approached, the excitement

crescendoed to insurmountable levels. Mom often made my

brother and me take what we called "Christmas walks"

to alleviate the tension. They almost always resulted in

some sort of mischief to shift the focus, if only for a

moment, from that incredible frenzy that would

begin again at dawn the next day.

Today I see that same anticipation in my own girls, though they seem to handle it with a more reserved finesse. The two older girls set the mood for the younger siblings through the decor, much like I used to, and the tradition of expectation continues. I imagine it's a taste of what Mary and Joseph must have experienced as they took their own Christmas walk to Bethlehem. Though the rest of the world would not be celebrating the birth of their child, as would be the custom centuries later, they did approach that incredible birth with the knowledge that something extraordinary was about to happen. The God of all creation was coming to earth—through their child—to restore the relationship between God and His people. Their people had awaited His arrival from the beginning of time. Now the moment had come, and all of heaven teemed with the excitement of . . . well, of a child before Christmas.

The God of all Creation

It Came Upon the Midnight Clear

It came upon the midnight clear,

That glorious song of old,

From angels bending near the earth

To touch their harps of gold:

"Peace on the earth, goodwill to men,

From heaven's all-gracious King";

The world in solemn stillness lay

To hear the angels sing.

For lo, the days are hastening on,

By prophet bards foretold,

When with the ever-circling years

Comes round the age of gold;

When peace shall over all the earth

Its ancient splendors fling,

And the whole world give back the song

Which now the angels sing.

Child of Bethlehem!

It came upon the midnight clear,

That glorious song of old,

From angels bending near the earth

To touch their harps of gold:

"Peace on the earth, goodwill to men,

From heaven's all-gracious King."

"And I will put enmity

Between you and the woman,

And between your seed and her Seed;

He shall bruise your head,

And you shall bruise His heel."

GENESIS 3:15

But when the fullness of the time had come, God sent

forth His Son, born of a woman, born under the law,

to redeem those who were under the law, that we might

receive the adoption as sons.

GALATIANS 4:4-5

God sent forth His Son

I see Him, but not now;

I behold Him, but not near;

A Star shall come out of Jacob;

A Scepter shall rise out of Israel,

And batter the brow of Moab,

And destroy all the sons of tumult.

NUMBERS 24:17

A braham begot Isaac, Isaac begot Jacob, and Jacob begot

Judah and his brothers. . . . Now after Jesus was born in

Bethlehem of Judea . . . behold, wise men from the East

came to Jerusalem, saying, "Where is He who has been

born King of the Jews? For we have seen His star in the

East and have come to worship Him."

MATTHEW 1:2; 2:1-2

Bethlehem of Judea

Therefore the Lord Himself will give you a sign:

Behold, the virgin shall conceive and bear a Son,

and shall call His name Immanuel.

ISAIAH 7:14

Now in the sixth month the angel Gabriel was sent

by God to a city of Galilee named Nazareth, to a virgin

betrothed to a man whose name was Joseph, of the house

of David. The virgin's name was Mary. . . . Then the angel

said to her, "Do not be afraid, Mary, for you have found

favor with God. And behold, you will conceive in your

womb and bring forth a Son, and shall call His

name JESUS."

LUKE 1:26-27, 30-31

Immanuel

For unto us a Child is born,

Unto us a Son is given;

And the government will be upon His shoulder.

And His name will be called

Wonderful, Counselor, Mighty God,

Everlasting Father, Prince of Peace.

Of the increase of His government and peace

There will be no end,

Upon the throne of David and over His kingdom,

To order it and establish it with judgment and justice

From that time forward, even forever.

The zeal of the LORD of hosts will perform this.

ISAIAH 9:6-7

Prince of Peace

"He will be great, and will be called the Son of the

Highest; and the Lord God will give Him the throne

of His father David. And He will reign over the house

of Jacob forever, and of His kingdom there will be

no end."

LUKE 1:32-33

There shall come forth a Rod from the stem of Jesse,

And a Branch shall grow out of his roots.

The Spirit of the LORD shall rest upon Him,

The Spirit of wisdom and understanding,

The Spirit of counsel and might,

The Spirit of knowledge and of the fear of the LORD. . . .

And in that day there shall be a Root of Jesse,

Who shall stand as a banner to the people;

For the Gentiles shall seek Him,

And His resting place shall be glorious.

ISAIAH 11:1-2, 10

"He raised up for them David as king, to whom also He

gave testimony and said, 'I have found David the son of

Jesse, a man after My own heart, who will do all My will.'

From this man's seed, according to the promise,

God raised up for Israel a Savior—Jesus."

ACTS 13:22-23

Savior—Jesus

29

O Little Town of Bethlehem

O little town of Bethlehem,

How still we see thee lie!

Above thy deep and dreamless sleep

The silent stars go by;

Yet in thy dark streets shineth

The everlasting Light;

The hopes and fears of all the years

Are met in thee tonight.

O holy Child of Bethlehem!

Descend to us, we pray;

Cast out our sin and enter in,

Be born in us today.

We hear the Christmas angels

The great glad tidings tell;

O come to us, abide with us,

Our Lord Emmanuel!

Everlasting Light

O Little Town of Bethlehem

How still we see thee lie!

Above thy deep and dreamless sleep

The silent stars go by;

Yet in thy dark streets shineth

The everlasting Light.

Born Is the King

THE PROPHECY FULFILLED

The heart behind the greatest gift could
not be measured. God had given us His
very best—a part of Himself—and the
world would never be the same.

The Gift

The day had finally arrived. And it did not disappoint. I woke up my brother and sister, who also lay listless in bed, pretending to have slept. Together we rushed to the tree, and there in the glow of blinking lights shined three new bikes, glistening like dew in the early morning sun. I stood amazed at how mom seemed to always find a way through the poverty to make us smile. Later, through a friend, I discovered she had received the bikes from the sheriff through an underprivileged child program. Kevin, my friend who reported these facts, said, "Hey, man, I didn't know you were underprivileged." I said, "I didn't know I was either."

But we did know that buying good gifts wasn't easy, so we had to work hard and pool our resources together to get mom the present she really wanted. One year it was a recliner. Mom would work long, hard days at the county clerk's office, and after cooking dinner for us, would collapse in front of the T.V. to relax. On that one Christmas morning, when we pulled the recliner out from its hiding place, we saw the delight in mother's eyes that we knew she always found in ours. What a success!

But the most treasured gifts were the ones we made, the ones that revealed our hearts. I even appreciated (though admittedly, halfheartedly) the chartreuse green sweater my mother had spent a year knitting for me, knowing that despite its appearance it was from a well-meaning source. The same for the set of mile-long scarves she made that literally wound around my entire body like an oversized turban. I, of course, often drew pictures for my brother and sister, buying the frame at a nearby five-and-dime

store. They, in turn, came up with their own creativity, and where money lacked for powerful show, laughter and joy filled in its place, always making Christmas merry for all of us.

I guess, in retrospect, we could have been discouraged or depressed because our lives fell short of the material standard seen in society today. But we chose laughter and joy instead, in its most old-fashioned, almost backward style, and we found a love and hope that riches can't buy.

Our Christmas gift-giving was similar to the way our heavenly Father presented us with the greatest gift in the world. The package was certainly less than spectacular. He sent His own Son—fully God—to earth as a tiny little baby, born to nondescript parents in a forsaken barn. Cold and alone, they wrapped Him in strips of cloth and laid Him in the same manger that fed the cows and donkeys nearby. But the heart behind the gift could not be measured. God had given us His very best—a part of Himself— and the world would never be the same. In its material splendor, the world failed to find reason to rejoice, but heaven saw the heart

behind the gift, and celebrated with the loudest chorus of praise,

"Glory to God in the highest,

And on earth peace, goodwill toward men!"

Glory to God

The First Noel

The first noel the angel did say
Was to certain poor shepherds in fields as they lay—
In fields where they lay keeping their sheep,
On a cold winter's night that was so deep.
Noel, noel! Noel, noel!
Born is the King of Israel!

Then let us all with one accord
Sing praises to our heavenly Lord,
That hath made heaven and earth of naught,
And with His blood mankind hath bought.
Noel, noel! Noel, noel!
Born is the King of Israel!

Noel, noel! Noel, noel!

Was to certain poor shepherds
in fields as they lay—

Noel, noel!

In fields where they lay

keeping their sheep,

On a cold winter's night that was so deep.

Born is the King of Israel!

Now in the sixth month the angel Gabriel was sent by God to a city of Galilee named Nazareth, to a virgin betrothed to a man whose name was Joseph, of the house of David. The virgin's name was Mary. And having come in, the angel said to her, "Rejoice, highly favored one, the Lord is with you; blessed are you among women!" But when she saw him, she was troubled at his saying, and considered what manner of greeting this was. Then the angel said to her, "Do not be afraid, Mary, for you have found favor with God. And behold, you will conceive in your womb and bring forth a Son, and shall call His name JESUS. He will be great, and will be called the Son of the Highest; and the Lord God will give Him the throne of His father David. And He will reign over the house of Jacob forever, and of His kingdom there will be no end."

LUKE 1:26-33

Rejoice

Now the birth of Jesus Christ was as follows: After His mother Mary was betrothed to Joseph, before they came together, she was found with child of the Holy Spirit. Then Joseph her husband, being a just man, and not wanting to make her a public example, was minded to put her away secretly. But while he thought about these things, behold, an angel of the Lord appeared to him in a dream, saying, "Joseph, son of David, do not be afraid to take to you Mary your wife, for that which is conceived in her is of the Holy Spirit. And she will bring forth a Son, and you shall call His name JESUS, for He will save His people from their sins."

MATTHEW 1:18-21

Do not be afraid

And it came to pass in those days that a decree went out from Caesar Augustus that all the world should be registered. This census first took place while Quirinius was governing Syria. So all went to be registered, everyone to his own city. Joseph also went up from Galilee, out of the city of Nazareth, into Judea, to the city of David, which is called Bethlehem, because he was of the house and lineage of David, to be registered with Mary, his betrothed wife, who was with child. So it was, that while they were there, the days were completed for her to be delivered. And she brought forth her firstborn Son, and wrapped Him in swaddling cloths, and laid Him in a manger, because there was no room for them in the inn.

Luke 2:1-7

Firstborn Son

*N*ow there were in the same country shepherds living out in the fields, keeping watch over their flock by night. And behold, an angel of the Lord stood before them, and the glory of the Lord shone around them, and they were greatly afraid. Then the angel said to them, "Do not be afraid, for behold, I bring you good tidings of great joy which will be to all people. For there is born to you this day in the city of David a Savior, who is Christ the Lord. And this will be the sign to you: You will find a Babe wrapped in swaddling cloths, lying in a manger." And suddenly there was with the angel a multitude of the heavenly host praising God and saying:

"Glory to God in the highest,

And on earth peace, goodwill toward men!"

So it was, when the angels had gone away from them into heaven, that the shepherds said to one another, "Let us now go to Bethlehem and see this thing that has come to pass, which the Lord has made known to us." And they came with haste and found Mary and Joseph, and the Babe lying in a manger.

LUKE 2:8-16

Peace

Now after Jesus was born in Bethlehem of Judea in the days of Herod the king, behold, wise men from the East came to Jerusalem, saying, "Where is He who has been born King of the Jews? For we have seen His star in the East and have come to worship Him." . . . Then Herod, when he had secretly called the wise men, determined from them what time the star appeared. And he sent them to Bethlehem and said, "Go and search carefully for the young Child, and when you have found Him, bring back word to me, that I may come and worship Him also." When they heard the king, they departed; and behold, the star which they had seen in the East went before them, till it came and stood over where the young Child was. When they saw the star, they rejoiced with exceedingly great joy. And when they had come into the house, they saw the young Child with Mary His mother, and fell down and worshiped Him. And when they had opened their treasures, they presented gifts to Him: gold, frankincense, and myrrh.

MATTHEW 2:1-2, 7-11

King of the Jews

Away in a Manger

Away in a manger, no crib for a bed,
The little Lord Jesus laid down His sweet head.
The stars in the sky looked down where He lay,
The little Lord Jesus, asleep on the hay.

Be near me, Lord Jesus! I ask Thee to stay
Close by me forever, and love me, I pray.
Bless all the dear children in Thy tender care,
And take us to heaven, to live with Thee there.

Away in a manger,

no crib for a bed,

The little Lord Jesus

laid down His sweet head.

Lord Jesus

The stars in the sky

looked down where He lay,

The little Lord Jesus,

asleep on the hay.

Joy to the World

LET HEAVEN AND NATURE SING!

Christmas is not necessarily about how beautiful you can make everything. It's about the heart attitude. It's like God's approach to us—He looks on the heart.

Thomas Kinkade

Pure Joy

To look at them, you might think you had stumbled across a more ragged version of the Beverly Hillbillies. Toothless, tattered, and very untrained, they broke into song:

"Joy to the world! The Lord is come;

Let earth receive her King;

Let every heart prepare Him room . . . ."

It was the annual caroling extravaganza of our little fundamental Nazarene group, and every home on the hillside fell victim to the Christmas cheer. This year the vagabond group gathered before our door, warming up only slightly off-key. My mom opened the door wide, revealing my own embarrassing appearance. I was covered with the measles and, consequently, wore sunglasses to protect my eyes. Donned with an old beanie cap and worn-out robe, I more than resembled the choir I faced. And face them I did—through all of the Christmas choruses you could ever care to remember.

It was as if, for this homely band of pilgrims, their joy would never run out. And despite its crude form, it was always contagious. Before long I would join in the throng, singing my heart out with the same abandon they demonstrated for me. And I realized, in that instant, that Christmas is not necessarily about how beautiful you can make everything. It's about the heart attitude. It's like God's approach to us—He looks on the heart.

I learned the same lesson a subsequent year, when mom took me with her to visit one of the members of our colorful congregation. We fondly called him the "amening" man. Every Sunday he'd shuffle to the back row of the church, take his seat, and wait for his cue. Deaf as a rock, we all wondered what his cue really was. But at about five minute intervals throughout the sermon, he'd rouse himself as if out of a slumber and shout, "Amen!" then settle back into obscurity. It was a wonderfully odd way of keeping us all awake.

This day, though, I saw him in a different light. My mom had heard he had a heart for cinnamon rolls. So she baked him a batch of her famous buns and set out for the one-room shack he called home. Seated next to the amening man was his fifty-year-old son, whose mental capacity fell far beneath his years. They both looked up, the man unable to hear what we said, and the son unable to understand why. But when my mom pulled out the cinnamon buns, the light of recognition, understanding, and joy ignited. And without a word, they heard the Christmas message loud and clear:

"Joy to the world! The Lord is come;

Let earth receive her King;

Let every heart prepare Him room,

And heaven and nature sing!"

I crawled into bed that night, singing the chorus, marveling at the different hearts where the King did find room. And I sang myself to sleep with a smile.

*And heaven
and nature sing!*

Joy to the World!

Joy to the world! The Lord is come;

Let earth receive her King;

Let every heart prepare Him room,

And heaven and nature sing,

And heaven and nature sing,

And heaven, and heaven and nature sing.

He rules the world with truth and grace,

And makes the nations prove

The glories of His righteousness,

And wonders of His love,

And wonders of His love,

And wonders, wonders of His love.

Joy to the world!

The Lord is come;

Let earth receive her King

Heaven and Nature Sing

Let every heart

prepare Him room,

And heaven and nature sing.

He rules the world

with truth and grace.

"*My* soul magnifies the Lord,

And my spirit has rejoiced in God my Savior. . . .

For He who is mighty has done great things for me,

And holy is His name."

LUKE 1:46-47, 49

Holy is His name

61

Thomas
Kinkade

Then the angel said to them, "Do not be afraid, for behold, I bring you good tidings of great joy which will be to all people. For there is born to you this day in the city of David a Savior, who is Christ the Lord."

LUKE 2:10-11

Good Tidings

And my soul shall be joyful in the LORD;

It shall rejoice in His salvation.

PSALM 35:9

His Salvation

*Y*ou will show me the path of life;

In Your presence is fullness of joy;

At Your right hand are pleasures forevermore.

PSALM 16:11

The Path of Life

$\mathcal{B}$ut let all those rejoice who put their trust in You;

Let them ever shout for joy, because You defend them;

Let those also who love Your name

Be joyful in You.

PSALM 5:11

Shout for Joy

What Child Is This?

What child is this, who, laid to rest,

On Mary's lap is sleeping?

Whom angels greet with anthems sweet,

While shepherds watch are keeping?

This, this is Christ the King,

Whom shepherds guard and angels sing;

Haste, haste to bring Him laud,

The Babe, the son of Mary.

So bring Him incense, gold, and myrrh,

Come peasant, king, to own Him;

The King of kings salvation brings,

Let loving hearts enthrone Him.

This, this is Christ the King,

Whom shepherds guard and angels sing;

Haste, haste to bring Him laud,

The Babe, the son of Mary.

Christ the King

What child is this,

who, laid to rest,

On Mary's lap is sleeping?

This, this is Christ the King,

Whom shepherds guard

and angels sing.

Worship
and Praise

GLORY TO THE NEWBORN KING!

God's light is the light that draws us from the darkness on cold Christmas nights to witness the warmth and beauty of Christ and His love in its brightest form.

Christmas Lights

My memories of growing up often flood my mind like the colors on my canvas. So much of what I encountered resurfaces again in my work, through slightly altered form—particularly the light of Christmastime.

In Placerville Christmas was a wonderful time of often frosty mornings. As I recall, it was never snowing, but it would be a very chilly morning, and there always seemed to be a perfect light at Christmas. I just remember this very distinctly. I would wake up with this feeling of anticipation in my heart—like the world looked brighter that day. Somehow the light was a little more brilliant, a little clearer. . . the air was crisper. And often-times I'd step outside the screened-door porch just to smell the air. It was a moment of magic.

Throughout the season this magic prevailed. In fact, my family always pursued it, piling in the old, black Ford station wagon to cruise the town looking for Christmas lights. We could always count on this one, beautiful Victorian house, because the owner always went absolutely nuts displaying lights. Having decided he would be the king of Christmas lights, he turned them all on, covering all the eaves and every single dormer, corner and window, with the entire house coming alive as a silhouette at night. It looked like someone had drawn the house with lights and had actually sketched in all the outlines. It was really quite beautiful. It sat way up on a hill, and you could see it from the main highway that ran through town. Each year the traffic piled up at this one point, as people slowed to see the Victorian house in all its brilliant splendor.

My wife and our four daughters continue the tradition, loading up the car every year to see familiar sites that set the season in motion. With or without snow, the effect of the lights always warms my soul.

I think of this because, when I work on my paintings, I have a real sense that a light from within is coming from the canvas. There's something emerging that I didn't put there, and it touches and heals people's hearts in ways I could never imagine. From their testimonies I realize God's light is at work through my paintings, shining into their souls. It is the light of His love. While I don't have the same advantage Mary and Joseph had on that first Christmas when they actually beheld the life of the Lord, I do have a sense that I can sit at the manger and watch the Light of Bethlehem unfold.

I believe it is the light that draws us from the darkness on cold Christmas nights to witness the warmth and beauty of Christ and His love in its brightest form.

Light of Bethlehem

Hark! The Herald Angels Sing

Hark! the herald angels sing,
"Glory to the newborn King;
Peace on earth, and mercy mild,
God and sinners reconciled!"
Joyful, all ye nations, rise,
Join the triumph of the skies;
With the angelic host proclaim,
"Christ is born in Bethlehem!"
Hark! the herald angels sing,
"Glory to the newborn King."

Hail the heaven-born Prince of Peace!
Hail the Son of Righteousness!
Light and life to all He brings,
Risen with healing in His wings.
Mild He lays His glory by,
Born that man no more may die;
Born to raise the sons of earth,
Born to give them second birth.
Hark! the herald angels sing,
"Glory to the newborn King."

The Newborn King

Hark! the herald angels sing,

"Glory to the newborn King;

Peace on earth,

and mercy mild,

God and sinners reconciled!"

I will praise the LORD according to His righteousness,

And will sing praise to the name of the LORD Most High.

PSALM 7:17

Righteousness

Your mercy, O LORD, is in the heavens;

Your faithfulness reaches to the clouds.

Your righteousness is like the great mountains;

Your judgments are a great deep;

O LORD, You preserve man and beast.

PSALM 36:5-6

Faithfulness

I will praise You, O Lord, among the peoples;

I will sing to You among the nations.

For Your mercy reaches unto the heavens,

And Your truth unto the clouds.

Be exalted, O God, above the heavens;

Let Your glory be above all the earth.

PSALM 57:9-11

Mercy

Thomas Kinkade

I will praise the name of God with a song,

And will magnify Him with thanksgiving. . . .

Let heaven and earth praise Him,

The seas and everything that moves in them.

PSALM 69:30, 34

Thanksgiving

Praise the LORD!

Praise the LORD from the heavens;

Praise Him in the heights!

Praise Him, all His angels;

Praise Him, all His hosts!

Praise Him, sun and moon;

Praise Him, all you stars of light!

Praise Him, you heavens of heavens,

And you waters above the heavens!

Let them praise the name of the LORD,

For He commanded and they were created.

PSALM 148:1-5

Praise!

Silent Night, Holy Night

Silent night, holy night,
  All is calm, all is bright;
  Round yon Virgin Mother and Child,
  Holy Infant so tender and mild,
  Christ the Savior is born,
  Christ the Savior is born.

Silent night, holy night,
  Wondrous Star, lend thy light;
  With the angels let us sing
  Alleluia to our King!
  Christ the Savior is born,
  Christ the Savior is born.

Silent night, holy night,

All is calm, all is bright;

Christ the Savior is born.

Holy Night

Silent night, holy night,

Wondrous Star, lend thy light;

With the angels let us sing

Alleluia to our King!

Come Let Us Adore Him

GLORY TO GOD IN THE HIGHEST!

May the love of Jesus kindle a flame in your heart that brightens your world and beckons others to come and adore Him—Christ the Lord.

A Christmas Blessing

The greatest blessing, I believe, a person can extend to another is love—the very dimension of life that Christmas celebrates. Love is the time in our lives when we say to our heart, "Be still. You're at peace." Then we have the freedom to reach out and give of ourselves to the people nearby. When I reached that point in my own life, my work took on a whole new look.

I'm known as the painter of light, and people see the reason why. But what they might miss behind the light is my expression of love. It's the love relationship I have with the collectors and, hopefully, for the readers of this book. When they look at the painting and the book, I hope they feel the love that I have poured into these paintings as an anonymous act of service.

I see it as similar to instances where people have left behind a little pamphlet for another person to pick up. When I walk up and open that note, I become a recipient of that person's love and concern—a true extension of Jesus' love to me. And I try to do that with my paintings. I rarely, if ever, get a chance to meet the individuals who purchase the paintings or hang them on the walls of their home. But my work, my heart for them, becomes a part of their family, a part of their lives. And it is a hope and blessing that is passed from generation to generation.

There is also a great love in my heart for each person who would share the light of Christ with others, even as I have shared it with them. The world is so full of darkness. If we can, together, light a candle in our hearts—if enough people light that candle—the world would be a much brighter place.

The light, after all, is the spirit of Christmas. It is the light of the star that shined over Bethlehem, welcoming all to worship the King. It is the light of the angels and the chorus of heaven, praising God for His grace come to earth. It is the lights we see entwined around the tree and people's homes at

Christ the Lord

Christmas, and the warm glow in the windows from the fire inside. God's hope is our light. And the light of Christmas is His Son. May you and all you know experience the love of Jesus this Christmas. And may it kindle a flame in your heart that brightens your world and beckons others to come and adore Him—Christ the Lord.

> "O come, let us adore Him,
>
> O come, let us adore Him,
>
> O come, let us adore Him,
>
> Christ, the Lord."

O Come, All Ye Faithful

O come, all ye faithful, joyful and triumphant,

O come ye, O come ye to Bethlehem;

Come and behold Him, born the King of angels;

O come, let us adore Him,

O come, let us adore Him,

O come, let us adore Him, Christ, the Lord.

Sing, choirs of angels, sing in exultation,

O sing, all ye citizens of heaven above;

Glory to God, all glory in the highest;

O come, let us adore Him,

O come, let us adore Him,

O come, let us adore Him, Christ, the Lord.

O come, all ye faithful,

joyful and triumphant,

O come ye,

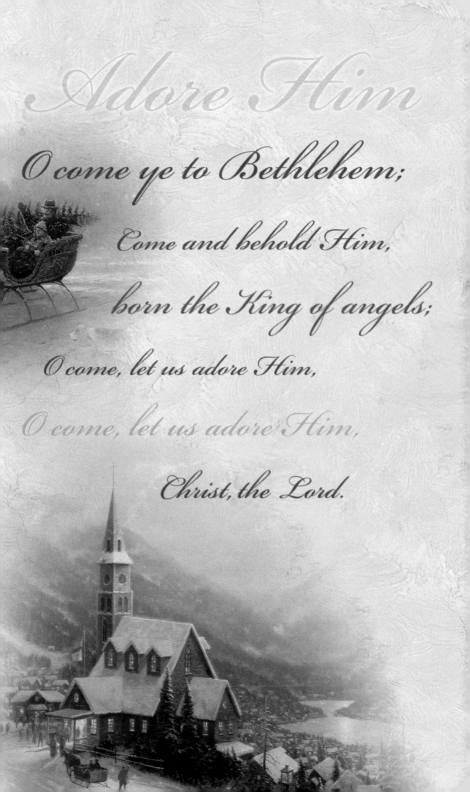

Adore Him

O come ye to Bethlehem;

Come and behold Him,

born the King of angels;

O come, let us adore Him,

O come, let us adore Him,

Christ, the Lord.

His name shall endure forever;

His name shall continue as long as the sun.

And men shall be blessed in Him;

All nations shall call Him blessed.

Blessed be the LORD God, the God of Israel,

Who only does wondrous things!

And blessed be His glorious name forever!

And let the whole earth be filled with His glory.

Amen and Amen.

PSALM 72:17-19

Amen

Oh come, let us worship and bow down;

Let us kneel before the LORD our Maker.

For He is our God,

And we are the people of His pasture,

And the sheep of His hand.

PSALM 95:6-7

He is our God

Thomas Kinkade

And the Word became flesh and dwelt among us,
and we beheld His glory, the glory as of the only
begotten of the Father, full of grace and truth.

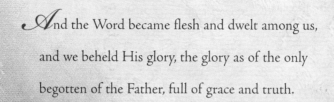

JOHN 1:14

Grace and Truth

Therefore God also has highly exalted Him and given Him the name which is above every name, that at the name of Jesus every knee should bow, of those in heaven, and of those on earth, and of those under the earth, and that every tongue should confess that Jesus Christ is Lord, to the glory of God the Father.

PHILIPPIANS 2:9-11

Highly Exalted

"Worthy is the Lamb who was slain

To receive power and riches and wisdom,

And strength and honor and glory and blessing!"

And every creature which is in heaven and on the earth

and under the earth and such as are in the sea,

and all that are in them, I heard saying:

"Blessing and honor and glory and power

Be to Him who sits on the throne,

And to the Lamb, forever and ever!"

REVELATION 5:12-13

Honor and Glory

Who Is He?

Who is He in yonder stall,

At whose feet the shepherds fall?

Who is He in deep distress,

Fasting in the wilderness?

'Tis the Lord! O wondrous story!

'Tis the Lord! the King of glory!

At His feet we humbly fall,

Crown Him! crown Him, Lord of all!

Who is He that from the grave

Comes to heal and help and save?

Who is He that from His throne

Rules through all the world alone?

'Tis the Lord! O wondrous story!

'Tis the Lord! the King of glory!

At His feet we humbly fall,

Crown Him! crown Him, Lord of all!

'Tis the Lord!

Who is He that from His throne

Rules through all the world alone?

'Tis the Lord! O wondrous story!

'Tis the Lord! the King of glory!

At His feet we humbly fall,

Crown Him! crown Him, Lord of all!

Special Christmas Memories